THANK YOU!

FOR CHOOSING

FOOTBALL
ACTIVITY BOOK
FOR KIDS

We value your opinion and would appreciate your feedback.

Your insights can help us improve future publications and

enhance the customer experience. Thank you for taking the

time to share your thoughts with us.

FOOTBALL

ACTIVITY BOOK FOR KIDS

EURO 24 EDITION

FOOTBALL
ACTIVITY BOOK

FOR KIDS

TABLE OF CONTENTS

TABLE OF CONTENTS

THIS BOOK BELONGS TO

EURO 24 EDITION

INTRODUCTION

Welcome to the 'Football Activity Book' – an exciting journey into the world of football, where fun meets learning! This book is divided into two sections, each packed with a variety of engaging activities tailored for young football enthusiasts.

In the first section, dive into the thrilling universe of football with activities like colouring, word searches, crosswords, boggled puzzles, word scrambles, math puzzles, mazes, and much more. These activities are not only entertaining but also sneak in a bit of education and challenges for young minds.

The second section is an exclusive treat for football lovers – the 'Euro 24 Special Edition.' Immerse yourself in the excitement of Euro 24 with specially crafted activities that celebrate the spirit of this grand football event. From colouring your favourite teams to navigating through football-themed mazes, this special edition brings an extra dose of football fun.

Get ready to explore, learn, and have a blast with the Football Activity Book. It's the perfect companion for young fans who want to combine their love for football with hours of delightful activities!

ABOUT ME

NAME

_____

AGE

_____

I LIVE WITH

_____

I LOVE TO PLAY

_____

ABOUT ME

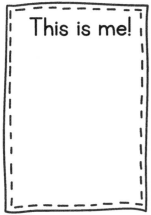

This is me!

Let's get to know you better. Fill in the shapes with your favourite things and share your awesome favourites with us.

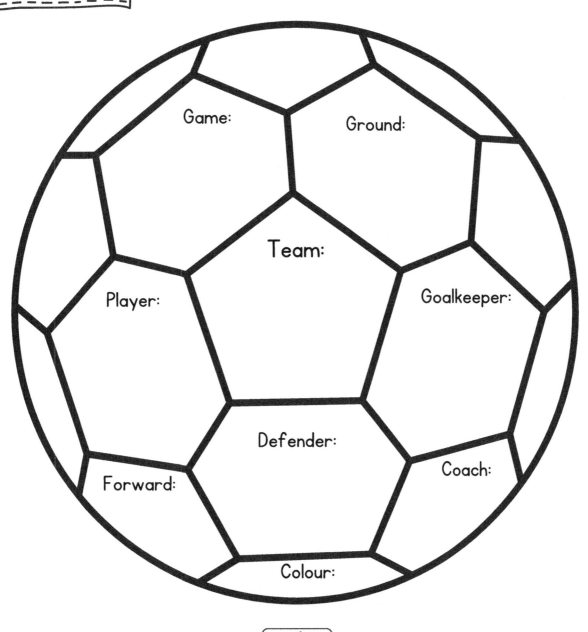

Game:

Ground:

Team:

Player:

Goalkeeper:

Defender:

Forward:

Coach:

Colour:

STARTING LINE UP

Time to build your dream team! Line up your players and write down the names of your favourite football stars in each position. Don't forget to add their jersey numbers! Imagine the excitement as your dream team takes the field. Ready to create some magic? Let's go!

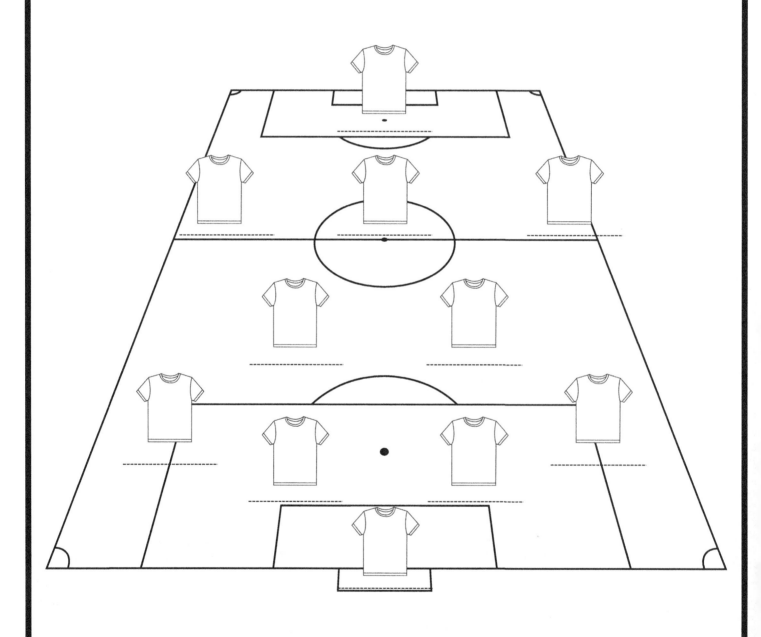

FUN COLOURING

Colour the picture of the boy playing football.

Make the sky blue, the grass green, and use fun colours for his clothes,

shoes, the football, and anything else you want to add! Have fun!

6

FUN COLOURING

Colour the picture of the boy going to play football.
Make the sky blue, the grass green, and use fun colours for her clothes,
football kit, shoes, the football, and anything else you want to add.

FUN COLOURING

Colour the picture of the boy playing football.
Make the sky blue, the grass green, and use fun colours for his clothes,
shoes, the football, and anything else you want to add! Have fun!

FUN COLOURING

Colour the picture of the boy playing football.
Make the sky blue, the grass green, and use fun colours for his clothes,
shoes, the football, and anything else you want to add! Have fun!

FUN COLOURING

Colour the picture of the girl playing football.

Make the sky blue, the grass green, and use fun colours for her clothes,

shoes, the football, and anything else you want to add! Have fun!

FUN COLOURING

Colour the picture of the girl playing football.
Make the sky blue, the grass green, and use fun colours for her clothes,
shoes, the football, and anything else you want to add! Have fun!

FAVOURITE PLAYER

Colour your favourite Football Player

DESIGN YOUR OWN T-SHIRT

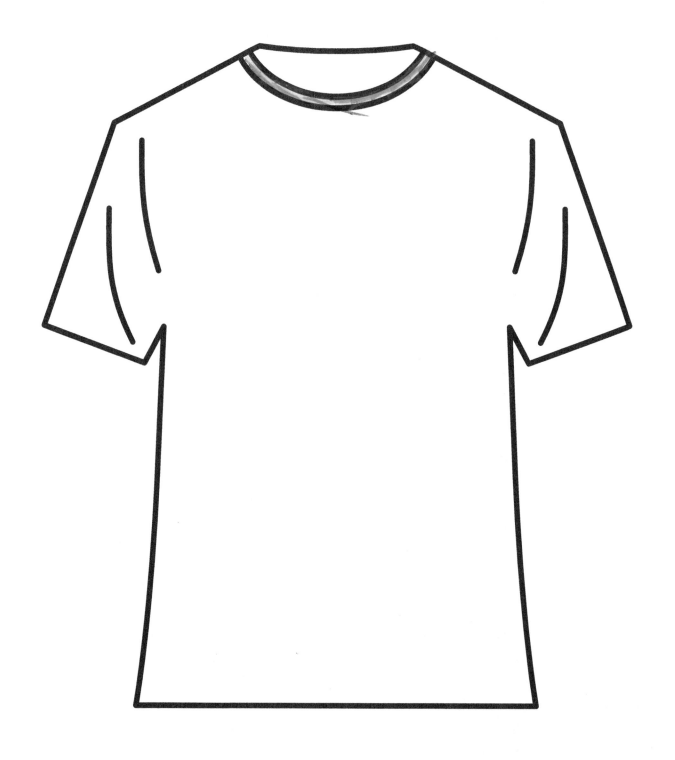

DESIGN YOUR GLOVES

DESIGN YOUR FOOTBALL EQUIPMENT

MAZE #1

Navigate the maze, avoid obstacles, and
kick goals past the goalie

18

MAZE #2

Dribble through the maze, skillfully avoiding obstacles, and aim to score a goal

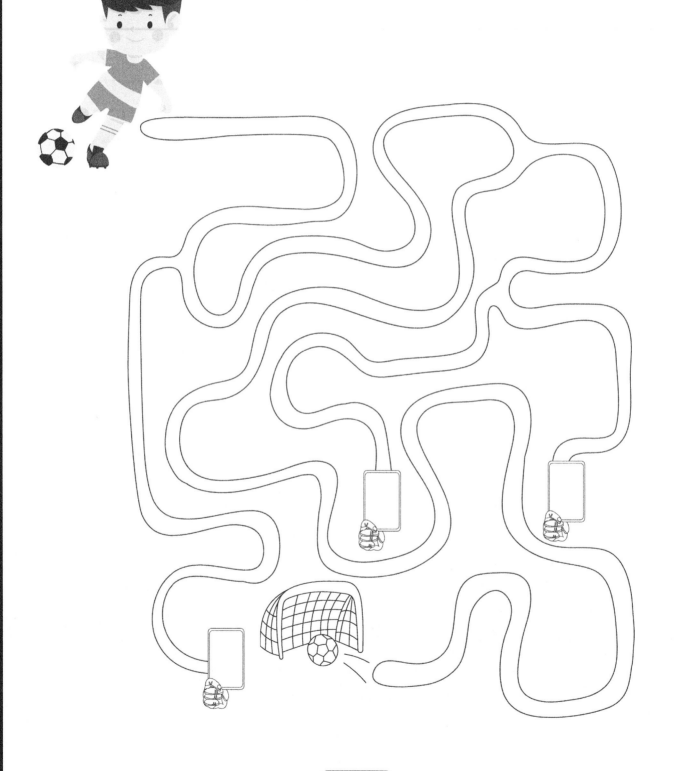

MAZE #3

Pass the ball through the maze to your teammate,
communicate, navigate obstacles with teamwork.

MAZE #4

Can you help the boy find his way to the pitch? Guide him through the maze.

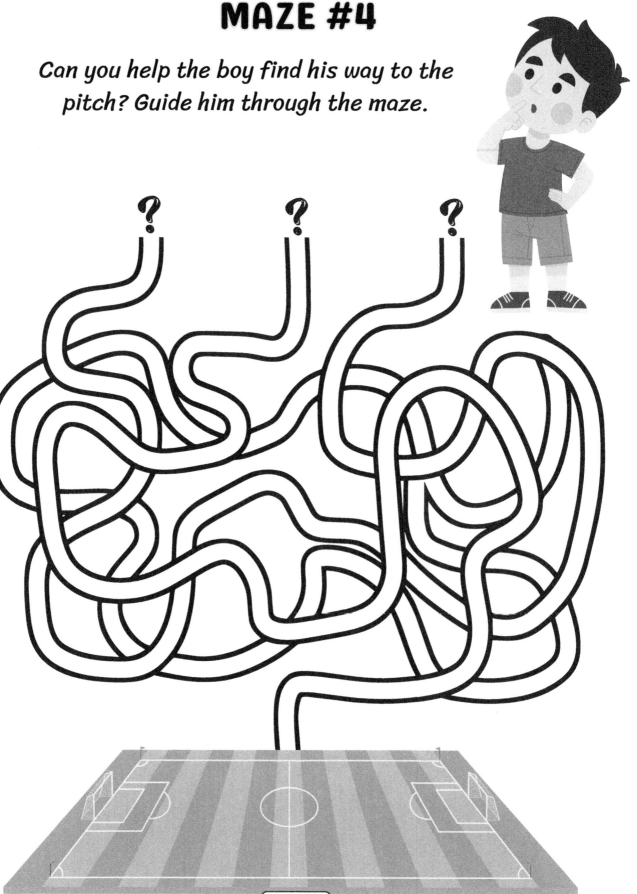

MAZE #5

Find your way through the maze to reach the Football

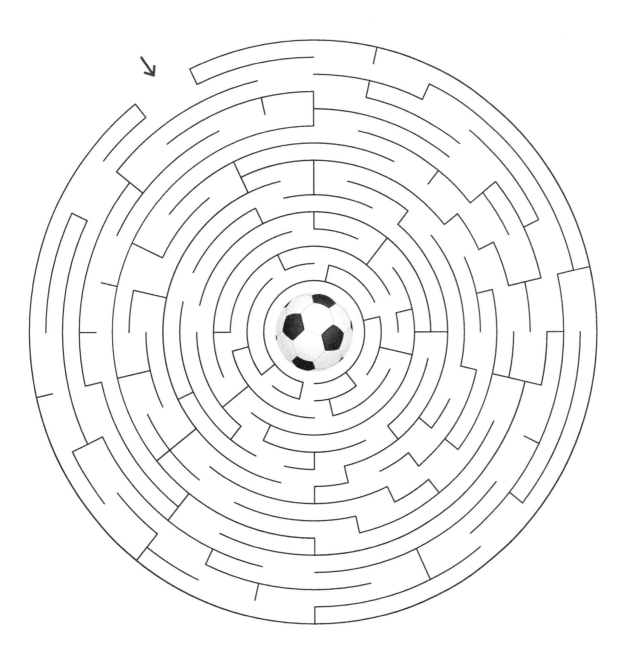

MAZE #6

Navigate the maze, collect footballs by following the
arrows, reach the net and score goals.

BOGGLED PUZZLE

Boggled puzzles are super fun! All you have to do is find lots of little words that are 3 letters or more. Here's how you play: look at the grid of letters. You can start your word anywhere and connect letters that are next to each other. You can go up and down, side to side, or even diagonally.

SCORING

3 letters	=	1 point	6 letters	=	4 point
4 letters	=	2 points	7 letters	=	5 points
5 letters	=	3 points	8 + letters	=	6 points

T	C	C	K	M
O	I	H	A	T
P	L	L	E	V
F	A	S	A	O
B	Y	W	G	L

MY SCORE

MY SCORE

24

BOGGLED PUZZLE

Boggled puzzles are super fun! All you have to do is find lots of little words that are 3 letters or more. Here's how you play: look at the grid of letters. You can start your word anywhere and connect letters that are next to each other. You can go up and down, side to side, or even diagonally.

SCORING

3 letters	=	1 point	6 letters	=	4 point
4 letters	=	2 points	7 letters	=	5 points
5 letters	=	3 points	8 + letters	=	6 points

Y	L	B	W	I
L	A	O	U	N
P	S	G	R	I
A	S	K	T	E
K	I	C	M	A

MY SCORE

MY SCORE

25

BOGGLED PUZZLE

Boggled puzzles are super fun! All you have to do is find lots of little words that are 3 letters or more. Here's how you play: look at the grid of letters. You can start your word anywhere and connect letters that are next to each other. You can go up and down, side to side, or even diagonally.

SCORING

3 letters	=	1 point		6 letters	=	4 point
4 letters	=	2 points		7 letters	=	5 points
5 letters	=	3 points		8 + letters	=	6 points

S	C	Z	F	D
H	O	R	I	L
F	T	N	E	B
I	E	T	U	H
M	A	R	C	S

MY SCORE

MY SCORE

26

WORD SCRAMBLE #1

Little football fan! Are you ready for a super fun challenge? Try unscrambling these 10 football-related words in our awesome football anagram puzzle!

RDE   ☐☐☐

USB   ☐☐☐

NOZE   ☐☐☐☐

ARDW   ☐☐☐☐

STOH   ☐☐☐☐

SVAE   ☐☐☐☐

SOTS   ☐☐☐☐

HCTIP   ☐☐☐☐☐

TOWHR   ☐☐☐☐☐

LRILD   ☐☐☐☐☐

WORD SCRAMBLE #2

Little football fan! Are you ready for a super fun challenge? Try unscrambling these 10 football-related words in our awesome football anagram puzzle!

NRRCEO

ALSETC

WEYLOL

ERAHED

LRIEDBB

EECFDNE

ODFEFSI

ERRFEEE

OCFEEFN

HEAFMLTI

WORD SEARCH #1

Can you find the words below hidden in the grid? Words can be found horizontally, vertically, or diagonally. Keep an eye out in all directions!

R	A	D	D	Z	H	A	R	S	O	Y	X	D	O	D
B	E	R	H	E	O	R	E	L	M	U	D	X	I	R
H	S	K	A	T	D	P	D	Y	A	Q	E	E	O	I
T	L	D	I	U	J	O	N	G	Y	P	P	D	I	B
Y	E	U	T	R	I	Z	E	B	U	C	L	C	K	B
R	H	O	O	G	T	U	F	B	K	E	S	I	E	L
T	C	Z	C	F	E	S	E	P	I	G	C	D	K	E
M	E	Y	P	L	M	Z	D	F	E	K	N	D	U	Y
D	T	N	K	G	H	O	D	B	O	N	B	N	G	V
C	T	R	G	D	V	I	R	F	D	D	A	A	E	X
H	F	K	Y	B	M	G	F	A	I	B	U	L	P	Q
V	Y	M	W	A	P	O	F	F	S	I	D	E	T	V
V	F	F	O	C	F	A	Z	R	U	C	O	Z	M	Y
X	T	C	Z	Q	Y	L	E	E	R	E	F	E	R	R
U	W	C	X	U	W	R	F	Y	U	H	C	T	I	P

PITCH	**KICKOFF**	**DEFENDER**	**PENALTY**
FOUL	**REFEREE**	**MIDFIELD**	**DRIBBLE**
GOAL	**STRIKER**	**OFFSIDE**	**HEADER**

WORD SEARCH #2

Can you find the words below hidden in the grid? Words can be found horizontally, vertically, or diagonally. Keep an eye out in all directions!

P	B	G	R	N	I	N	L	S	V	W	D	N	B	T
Q	R	C	Q	L	I	T	E	V	A	U	L	O	O	M
S	T	A	E	L	C	A	G	G	P	J	F	I	O	X
T	J	S	E	I	N	Q	T	M	S	P	U	T	K	F
A	D	N	I	S	U	P	F	P	G	J	M	U	I	I
T	P	B	C	A	Q	V	I	V	A	S	F	T	N	G
C	I	S	F	S	J	L	O	T	S	C	S	I	G	W
V	R	X	E	A	I	L	N	O	C	C	L	T	I	B
O	R	Z	Z	V	L	X	R	T	O	H	H	S	U	Q
C	O	R	N	E	R	C	X	R	A	L	H	B	T	B
F	M	H	Y	C	N	R	E	C	S	C	O	U	X	W
H	A	T	T	R	I	C	K	F	N	M	K	S	O	I
Q	R	A	A	S	M	M	C	D	V	E	P	L	S	W
F	I	O	P	U	X	I	T	X	E	H	H	R	E	K
M	F	R	U	X	H	J	A	Z	Q	P	A	R	R	U

CORNER	SCORE	SUBSTITUTION	PITCH
TACKLE	CLEATS	CROSS	BOOKING
SAVE	CAPTAIN	HAT-TRICK	VOLLEY

WORD SEARCH #3

Can you find the words below hidden in the grid? Words can be found horizontally, vertically, or diagonally. Keep an eye out in all directions!

```
W  Q  C  C  T  D  C  O  K  L  C  N  I  I  U
R  H  L  R  N  J  I  F  C  X  E  A  G  N  K
M  X  I  O  E  G  R  S  I  T  K  D  G  J  C
G  V  D  S  P  U  Z  F  K  N  D  X  F  U  A
X  A  Z  S  T  B  W  Y  E  C  F  L  D  R  B
E  S  R  B  N  L  S  S  E  F  T  R  W  Y  L
T  J  M  A  T  O  E  M  R  W  A  A  C  T  L
U  O  L  R  F  J  I  N  F  C  L  E  J  I  U
Z  G  R  I  J  T  Y  T  W  L  R  H  P  M  F
N  I  D  N  F  Y  M  O  A  C  L  C  T  E  C
E  O  G  L  S  Y  L  U  X  M  Q  N  P  N  Y
K  H  A  L  C  L  A  K  W  X  R  O  Y  P  C
E  H  J  W  E  F  J  S  B  K  H  O  L  U  P
E  R  Q  Y  R  E  D  C  A  R  D  O  F  V  R
E  M  I  T  A  R  T  X  E  R  E  G  D  M  B
```

FREE-KICK	**WHISTLE**	**EXTRA TIME**	**HALFTIME**
YELLOW CARD	**CROSSBAR**	**FORMATION**	**INJURY TIME**
RED CARD	**NET**	**FULLBACK**	**WALL**

WORD SEARCH #4

Can you find the words below hidden in the grid? Words can be found horizontally, vertically, or diagonally. Keep an eye out in all directions!

G	B	V	J	Y	P	T	C	R	T	V	C	E	F	S
F	X	P	X	R	A	R	X	O	E	G	O	F	X	A
S	T	R	I	K	E	S	U	M	C	G	U	O	W	V
I	F	N	L	B	Z	C	C	R	J	E	N	Z	H	F
O	R	L	O	H	H	J	E	B	V	J	T	I	Z	W
D	W	U	I	L	W	P	D	B	Y	R	E	T	W	R
N	N	N	I	N	E	T	A	P	I	N	R	X	A	G
D	H	N	G	E	E	T	T	X	N	V	A	K	T	D
W	E	K	W	O	U	S	V	D	V	O	T	C	C	E
E	P	S	H	M	A	Q	M	V	L	L	T	I	U	E
N	D	L	B	O	L	L	T	A	H	L	A	L	O	Z
R	E	H	C	T	E	R	T	S	N	E	C	F	H	H
C	I	B	L	S	K	C	I	U	C	Y	K	O	H	X
A	N	G	J	T	P	K	V	V	Q	Z	P	V	N	U
O	M	P	L	S	W	D	R	L	V	Q	V	W	Q	V

TAP-IN	TOUCHLINE	FLICK	LINESMAN
OWN GOAL	STRETCHER	SWEEPER	VOLLEY
COUNTERATTACK	WINGER	STRIKES	REBOUND

WORD SEARCH #5

Can you find the words below hidden in the grid? Words can be found horizontally, vertically, or diagonally. Keep an eye out in all directions!

```
E  N  A  L  W  O  D  A  E  M  N  I  P  G  T
Z  T  J  N  R  E  Q  T  Y  X  K  D  I  S  H
X  Y  I  O  R  X  L  F  R  M  F  I  S  G  E
D  Q  H  A  B  L  P  A  H  Y  B  K  R  C  V
P  A  R  I  E  X  Y  X  D  M  W  P  V  I  A
A  V  H  W  V  I  L  L  A  P  A  R  K  T  L
Z  N  K  I  G  C  G  I  B  M  E  V  H  Y  L
Q  A  F  J  T  O  Y  M  F  V  M  E  S  G  E
O  X  T  I  L  E  V  X  J  T  D  J  D  R  Y
W  I  R  Z  E  B  M  P  Q  E  G  N  L  O  E
N  X  B  T  K  L  Q  Y  N  J  M  T  N  U  L
M  R  A  Y  B  O  D  G  G  U  I  X  T  N  B
K  R  A  P  T  S  R  U  H  L  E  S  N  D  M
T  Y  V  L  C  A  R  R  O  W  R  O  A  D  E
H  P  P  G  U  N  E  R  D  S  Z  H  U  S  W
```

OAKWELL	THE VALLEY	DEEPDALE	MEADOW LANE
VILLA PARK	THE DEN	CARROW ROAD	ETIHAD
ANFIELD	SELHURST PARK	CITY GROUND	WEMBLEY

WORD SEARCH #6

Can you find the words below hidden in the grid? Words can be found horizontally, vertically, or diagonally. Keep an eye out in all directions!

```
E  N  R  H  N  S  Z  F  I  I  W  S  S  R  H
C  W  E  Q  K  I  E  K  P  Z  N  E  T  E  A
I  A  E  D  W  Y  K  N  B  O  Z  E  L  I  R
R  Y  C  D  O  Z  L  H  O  R  X  Y  A  D  R
N  T  E  D  Q  F  V  E  I  T  M  I  K  C  Y
A  Q  J  W  U  Z  L  K  W  C  S  Q  Y  I  K
L  Q  A  M  B  J  O  I  H  A  W  N  B  R  A
C  Q  M  H  O  N  U  R  H  D  L  F  H  E  N
E  F  E  N  S  L  Y  V  E  P  X  K  H  O  E
D  R  S  A  N  Q  N  T  J  C  B  M  E  H  J
E  N  O  T  S  N  H  O  J  M  A  S  G  R  V
H  A  R  R  Y  M  A  G  U  I  R  E  C  S  I
C  A  L  L  U  M  W  I  L  S  O  N  Q  U  X
Q  W  N  M  D  G  E  S  E  I  M  K  K  L  J
S  P  I  L  L  I  H  P  N  I  V  L  A  K  M
```

REECE JAMES	**JOHN STONES**	**KYLE WALKER**	**PHIL FODEN**
EZRI KONSA	**ERIC DIER**	**HARRY KANE**	**DECLAN RICE**
SAM JOHNSTONE	**HARRY MAGUIRE**	**KALVIN PHILLIPS**	**CALLUM WILSON**

NUMBER 1 - 20

Fill each box with the correct spelling to solve the Crossword Puzzle. Pay close attention and use your super spelling skills.

COUNT AND MATCH

Circle the correct number of images

4   7   10

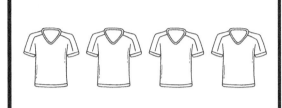

4   6   8

5   3   9

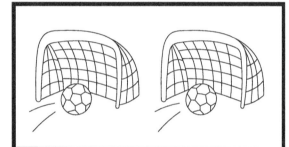

0   1   2

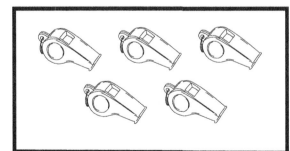

2   9   5

9   5   8

FOOTBALL COUNTING

Count the items and write the number in the box.

1.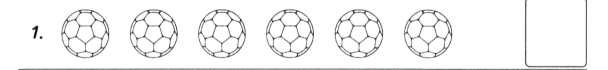

2.

3.

4.

5.

MATHS PUZZLE

Use your mathematical thinking skills to find the value of each image.

 + = 10

 + = 13

 + = 14

 + + =

Work Space

MATHS PUZZLE

Determine the value of each football item in the following maths problems.

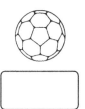 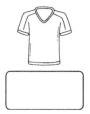 

 + = 10

 + = 12

 + = 4

 + =

 + + =

FOOTBALL GRAPHING

Find and graph the items listed. Then answer the questions below.

10
9
8
7
6
5
4
3
2
1

How many of each?

Which item did you find the most of?

_____

Which item did you find the least of?

_____

CROSSWORD #1

Fill in the crossword with words from the list below.

ACROSS

6. FORMATION

7. CAPTAIN

8. PENALTY KICK

10. FORWARD

12. MIDFIELDER

14. CORNER KICK

15. TACTICS

16. DEFENDER

DOWN

1. RED CARD

2. OFFSIDE

3. HEADER

4. GOALKEEPER

5. STRIKER

9. FREE KICK

11. YELLOW CARD

13. DRIBBLING

CROSSWORD #2

Fill in the crossword with words from the list below.

DOWN

1. SWEEPER

2. SUBSTITUTION

4. STOPPAGE TIME

5. CRUYFF TURN

6. HAT-TRICK

8. GOLDEN BOOT

10. RAINBOW FLICK

11. THROW-IN

14. NUTMEG

ACROSS

3. INJURY TIME

5. CLEAN SHEET

7. TIKI-TAKA

9. COUNTER ATTACK

12. BACK-HEEL

13. GOLDEN GLOVE

15. WALL

FOOTBALL MATCHING

Follow the trail and check all the football-related things. Don't forget to cross out anything that's not about football.

FOOTBALL MATCHING

Which two pictures are the same? Match them up!

FOOTBALL MATCHING

Which two pictures are the same? Match them up!

FOOTBALL MATCHING

Match the parts with correct pictures.

FIND THE ITEMS

Find and write the correct number of items below.

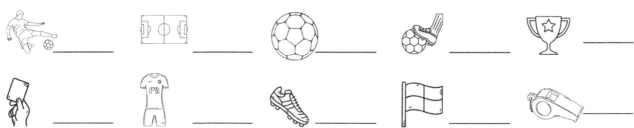

FIND THE ITEMS

Find and write the correct number of items below.

FOOTBALL QUIZ

Hello Football Champs! Read each question and circle the correct answer. Let's see how many goals (correct answers) you can score! Ready? Go!

What is the name of the game where players use their feet to kick a ball into the opponent's goal?

a. Basketball   b. Tennis   c. Football   d. Baseball

How many players are on a standard football (soccer) team during a game?

a. 8   b. 11   c. 15   d. 20

What do we call the player who guards the goal and tries to stop the opposing team from scoring?

a. Striker   b. Goalkeeper   c. Midfielder   d. Captain

Which part of the body is NOT allowed to touch the ball during a game (except for the goalkeeper)?

a. Head   b. Hands   c. Feet   d. Knees

What is it called when a player scores three goals in a single game?

a. Triple Score   b. Hat-trick   c. Goal Trio   d. Three-peat

---

What do players do when the ball goes out of bounds along the sidelines?

a. A free kick   b. A penalty kick   c. Throw-in   d. Goal kick

---

What is the term for the additional time added to the end of each half to make up for stoppages?

a. Extra Time   b. Bonus Time   c. Overtime   d. Injury Time

Which of the following is a foul in football?

a. Scoring a goal   b. Taking a throw-in   c. Pushing an opponent   d. Celebrating a win

---

What is the name of the line that the goalkeeper must stay behind when the opposing team takes a penalty kick?

a. Goal Line   b. Free-kick Line   c. Penalty Line   d. Touch Line

---

What do you call it when a player kicks the ball over their head and the opponent, also known as 'flipping' the ball?

a. Rainbow Flick   b. Sky Kick   c. Somersault Kick   d. Overhead Kick

49

SPOT THE DIFFERENCE

Spot 5 differences between the pictures

SPOT THE DIFFERENCE

Spot 10 differences between the pictures

SPOT THE DIFFERENCE

Spot 20 differences between the pictures

FOOTBALL DOT TO DOT

Get ready for some fun! Connect the dots to reveal the hidden picture. Imagine what it could be as you draw the lines. Let your creativity shine!

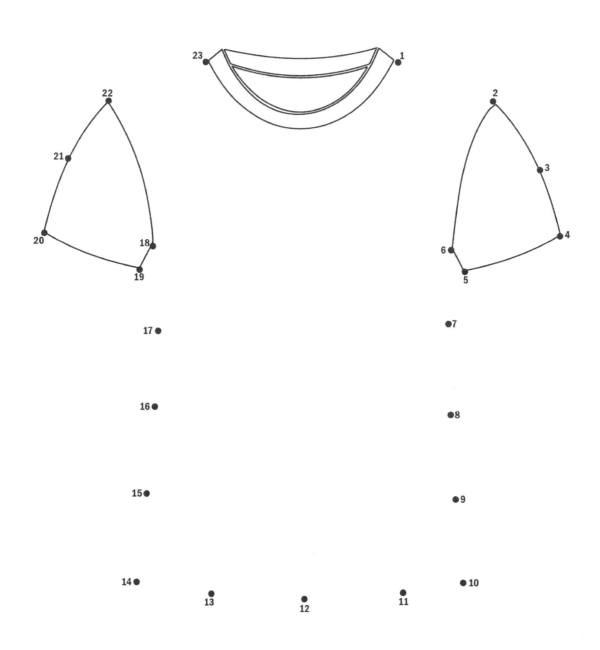

FOOTBALL DOT TO DOT

Get ready for some fun! Connect the dots to reveal the hidden picture. Imagine what it could be as you draw the lines. Let your creativity shine!

FOOTBALL DOT TO DOT

Get ready for some fun! Connect the dots to reveal the hidden picture. Imagine what it could be as you draw the lines. Let your creativity shine!

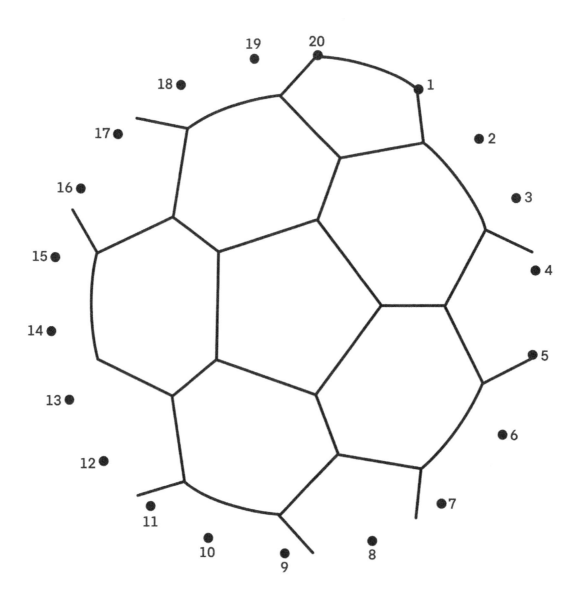

FOOTBALL DOT TO DOT

Get ready for some fun! Connect the dots to reveal the hidden picture. Imagine what it could be as you draw the lines. Let your creativity shine!

FOOTBALL DOT TO DOT

Get ready for some fun! Connect the dots to reveal the hidden picture. Imagine what it could be as you draw the lines. Let your creativity shine!

ANSWER KEYS

MAZE #1

MAZE #2

MAZE #3

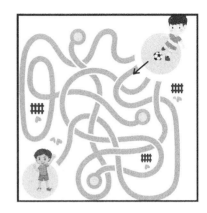

MAZE #4

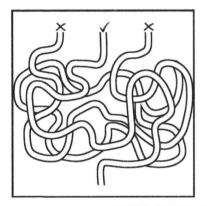

MAZE #5

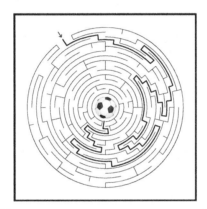

MAZE #6

WORD SCRAMBLE #1

RDE	RED
USB	SUB
NOZE	ZONE
ARDW	DRAW
STOH	SHOT
SVAE	SAVE
SOTS	TOSS
HCTIP	PITCH
TOWHR	THROW
LRILD	DRILL

WORD SCRAMBLE #2

NRRCEO	CORNER
ALSETC	CLEATS
WEYLOL	YELLOW
ERAHED	HEADER
LRIEDBB	DRIBBLE
EESFDNE	DEFENSE
ODFEFSI	OFFSIDE
ERRFEEE	REFEREE
OSFEEFN	OFFENSE
HEAFMLTI	HALFTIME

ANSWER KEYS

WORD SEARCH #1
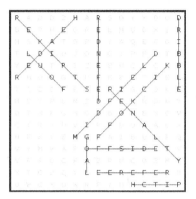

WORD SEARCH #2
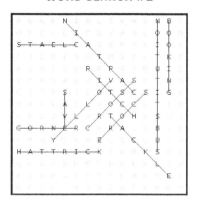

WORD SEARCH #3
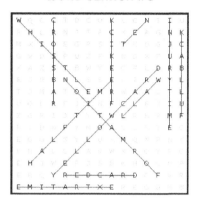

WORD SEARCH #4
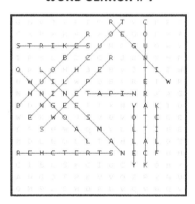

WORD SEARCH #5
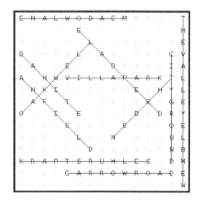

WORD SEARCH #6
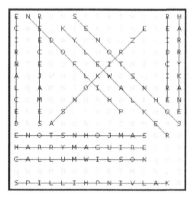

CROSSWORD #1
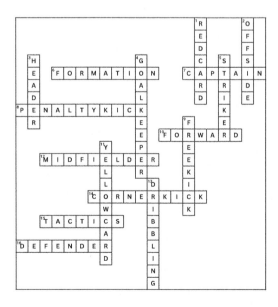

CROSSWORD #2

FOOTBALL QUIZ

1. C, 2. B, 3. B, 4. B, 5. B, 6. C, 7. A, 8. C, 9. C, 10. A

EURO 24 SPECIAL

Step into the 'Euro 24 Special'

A dedicated section in the 'Football Activity Book' designed for ultimate football fun!

Dive into colouring pages, puzzles, and challenges inspired by the excitement of Euro 24. Get ready to celebrate the tournament in a whole new way – it's football mania at your fingertips!

SECTION - 2

WHICH COUNTRY DO YOU SUPPORT?

ENGLAND

WHO IS YOUR FAVOURITE FOOTBALL PLAYER?

NAME

Halland

JERSEY NO

9

POSITION

St

WHO IS YOUR FAVOURITE GOALKEEPER?

EDeSon

DRAW AND COLOUR YOUR DREAM FOOTBALL PLAYER

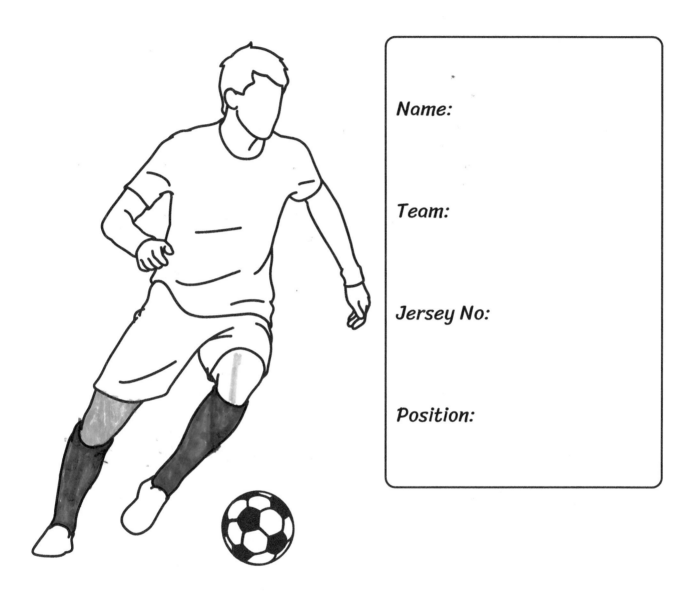

Name:

Team:

Jersey No:

Position:

Other Information

WHO HAS QUALIFIED FOR UEFA EURO 2024?

Austria	Albania	Belgium	Czechia
Croatia	England	Denmark	France
Germany	Hungary	Italy	Netherlands
Portugal	Romania	Scotland	Serbia
Slovakia	Slovenia	Spain	Switzerland
Turkey	Bosnia and Herzegovina	Estonia	Finland
Georgia	Greece	Iceland	Israel
Kazakhstan	Luxembourg	Poland	Ukraine
Wales	Andorra	Armenia	Azerbaijan
Belarus	Bulgaria	Cyprus	Faroe Islands
Gibraltar	Kosovo	Latvia	Liechtenstein
Lithuania	Malta	Moldova	Montenegro
North Macedonia	Northern Ireland	Norway	Republic of Ireland
	San Marino	Sweden	

FIRST PREDICTION

Time for some football fortune-telling! Make your own predictions by writing the names of teams you would like to see in the Quarter Final. Then, choose teams for the Semi Final, pick the finalists, and at last, decide which team will be the Euro 2024 champion. Let your football predictions unfold!

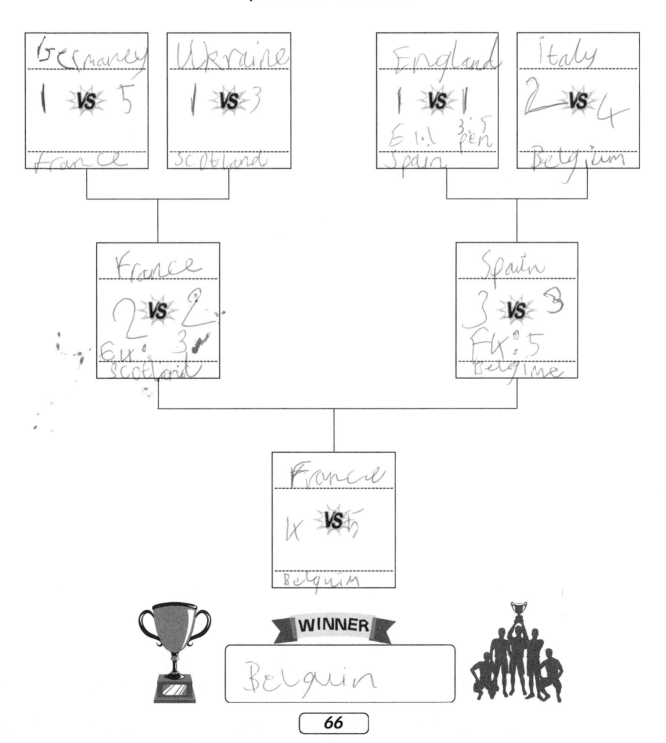

WINNER

Belgium

SECOND PREDICTION

Time for some football fortune-telling! Make your own predictions by writing the names of teams you would like to see in the Quarter Final. Then, choose teams for the Semi Final, pick the finalists, and at last, decide which team will be the Euro 2024 champion. Let your football predictions unfold!

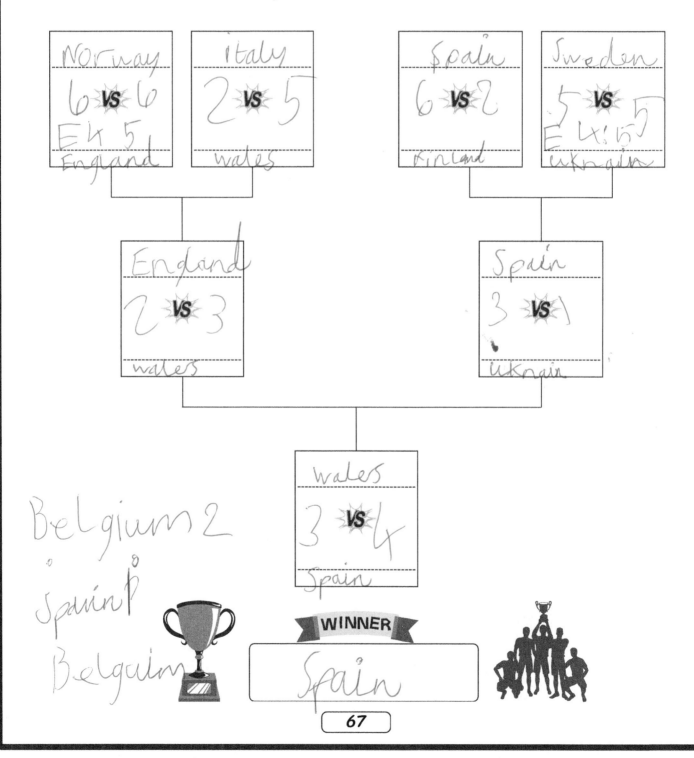

QUARTER FINAL

Norway	Italy	Spain	Sweden
6 VS 6	2 VS 5	6 VS 2	5 VS 5
E4 5			E 4:5
England	wales	Finland	ukrain

SEMI FINAL

England	Spain
2 VS 3	3 VS 1
wales	ukrain

FINAL

wales
3 VS 4
Spain

Belgium 2
Spain 0
Belguim

WINNER

Spain

COLOUR BY NUMBER

Get ready for a colourful adventure! Use the numbers to guide your colouring and create a fantastic country flag. Once you have added all the colours, write down the country's name.

1. Black   2. Red   3. White   4. Green   5. Yellow   6. Dark Blue

1
2
5

3
2

4	3	2

COLOUR BY NUMBER

Get ready for a colourful adventure! Use the numbers to guide your colouring and create a fantastic country flag. Once you have added all the colours, write down the country's name.

1. Black   2. Red   3. White   4. Green   5. Yellow   6. Dark Blue

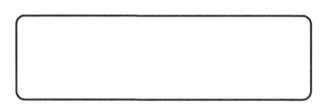

6	5	2

2
3
2

2
3
4

COLOUR BY NUMBER

Get ready for a colourful adventure! Use the numbers to guide your colouring and create a fantastic country flag. Once you have added all the colours, write down the country's name.

1. Black   2. Red   3. White   4. Green   5. Yellow   6. Dark Blue

6	5	2

2
3
2

2
3
4

MATCHING

Connect the flags to their countries on the map by drawing a line. Can you make all the right matches? Let's have some flag-matching fun!

MATCHING

Connect the flags to their countries name and map by drawing a line.
Can you make all the right matches?

 GERMANY

 SPAIN

 PORTUGAL

 ROMANIA

 POLAND

MATCHING

Connect the countries name to their map and flag by drawing a line.
Can you make all the right matches?

 **SWEDEN**

 **LATVIA**

 **SCOTLAND**

 **BELGIUM**

 **GREECE**

IDENTIFY COUNTRIES

Time to put your map skills to the test! Look at the map and write the names of the countries in the empty boxes. Can you fill in all the blanks correctly? Let's see your mapping magic!

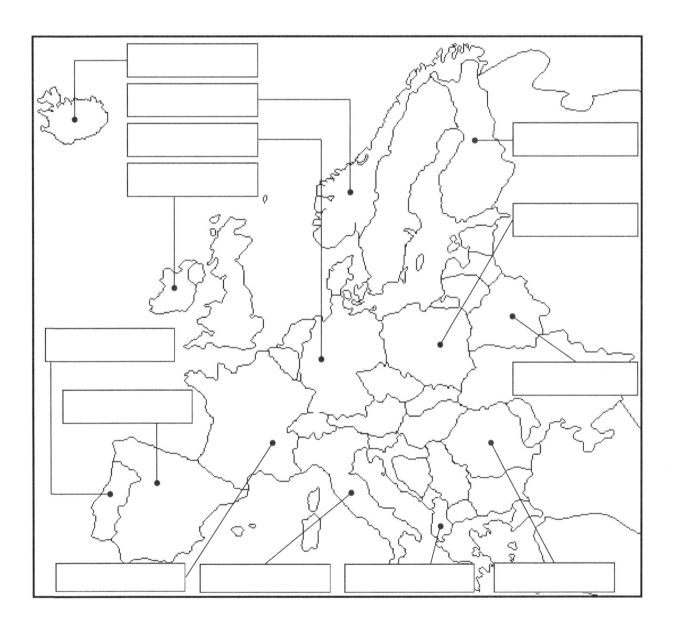

STADIUMS CHALLENGE

Can you match the stadium names to their correct locations or boxes?
Give it a try and see if you can place each stadium in its right spot.
Let the stadium fun begin!

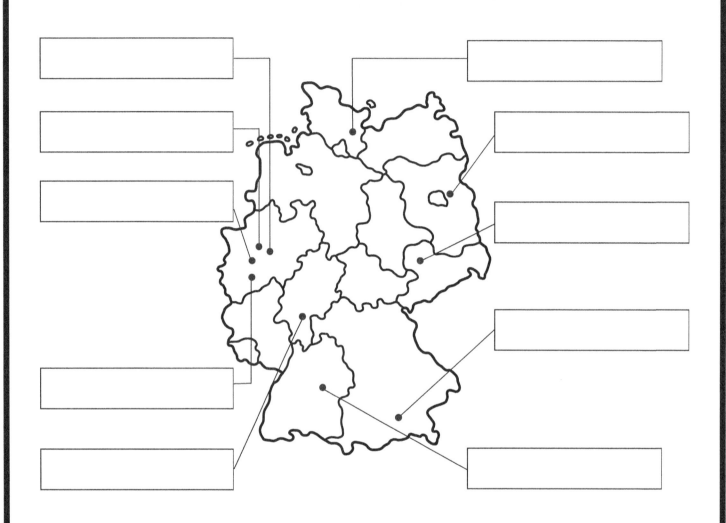

- DORTMUND
- GELSENKIRCHEN
- HAMBURG
- DÜSSELDORF
- COLOGNE
- FRANKFURT
- STUTTGART
- MUNICH
- LEIPZIG
- OLYMPIASTADION BERLIN

MATCHING

Let's play the matching game! Draw a line to match each player's name with their team. Can you make all the perfect matches?

JUDE BELLINGHAM	ARGENTINA
MOHAMED SALAH	SPAIN
LAUTARO MARTINEZ	ENGLAND
ERLING HAALAND	EGYPT
KYLIAN MBAPPE	NORWAY
RODRI	ENGLAND
HARRY KANE	FRANCE

MATCHING

Let's play the matching game! Draw a line to match each player's name with their team. Can you make all the perfect matches?

SERHOU GUIRASSY	PORTUGAL
SANTIAGO GIMENEZ	NIGERIA
CRISTIANO RONALDO	ENGLAND
JAMES MADDISON	GERMANY
VICTOR BONIFACE	MEXICO
DECLAN RICE	ENGLAND
LEROY SANE	GUINEA

EURO WORD SEARCH #1

Can you find the words below hidden in the grid? Words can be found horizontally, vertically, or diagonally. Keep an eye out in all directions!

P	Q	M	F	F	I	M	P	I	T	U	T	N	I	B
P	H	N	P	S	T	X	A	C	P	Y	R	G	Q	M
X	B	W	O	C	F	Y	W	I	N	E	E	Z	C	B
P	O	R	T	U	G	A	L	A	R	O	S	D	U	A
S	D	J	X	H	G	I	M	N	R	T	Z	F	A	I
J	L	R	Q	K	G	R	Q	G	S	D	S	K	V	T
T	O	O	Z	X	E	A	I	U	L	Z	D	U	C	A
U	X	D	V	G	Y	A	Q	B	F	M	X	J	A	O
R	S	Q	N	A	T	S	H	K	A	Z	A	K	M	R
K	X	E	C	I	K	V	O	G	F	D	F	M	R	C
E	M	U	L	K	T	I	V	D	J	P	W	C	W	B
Y	U	M	J	A	H	U	A	K	C	R	L	Y	W	R
O	S	Q	M	B	W	P	F	T	X	K	A	K	A	M
N	G	M	X	K	Z	W	W	W	D	T	S	U	S	B
T	T	P	R	O	U	G	N	K	N	W	M	H	G	S

AUSTRIA	PORTUGAL	GEORGIA
CROATIA	SLOVAKIA	KAZAKHSTAN
GERMANY	TURKEY	WALES

EURO WORD SEARCH #2

Can you find the words below hidden in the grid? Words can be found horizontally, vertically, or diagonally. Keep an eye out in all directions!

```
R  V  P  E  C  N  W  L  E  K  Y  X  L  A  Q
L  Q  R  T  G  N  C  N  U  Q  R  R  H  L  T
C  U  S  I  P  S  G  B  J  H  I  O  P  B  V
A  R  X  C  N  L  I  L  B  T  V  C  A  A  J
V  I  R  E  A  P  E  U  W  O  L  V  A  N  A
C  O  N  N  M  A  U  S  Y  K  R  E  I  I  I
G  A  D  A  I  B  G  R  E  E  C  E  F  A  N
A  N  Z  N  M  Z  O  L  Y  J  F  K  X  Z  E
Q  D  S  Q  Z  O  P  U  B  M  V  A  Y  P  V
R  O  T  W  V  D  R  Y  R  A  G  N  U  H  O
B  R  O  B  X  O  N  A  M  G  J  I  G  J  L
A  R  J  B  I  W  E  S  W  F  X  B  Q  N  S
V  A  I  P  A  R  H  Z  E  M  N  D  F  C  J
R  U  S  J  X  X  B  N  L  D  D  L  A  D  H
Q  R  W  O  Q  V  O  F  T  D  D  S  E  P  T
```

ALBANIA	ROMANIA	GREECE
ENGLAND	SLOVENIA	LUXEMBOURG
HUNGARY	BOSNIA	ANDORRA

EURO WORD SEARCH #3

Can you find the words below hidden in the grid? Words can be found horizontally, vertically, or diagonally. Keep an eye out in all directions!

```
G  S  D  Q  V  Y  O  A  V  V  Q  S  H  B  P
R  P  I  Q  K  V  I  O  G  H  Q  B  T  E  B
U  Z  J  W  W  N  I  H  R  C  S  S  D  D  D
X  F  K  S  E  U  Z  M  U  I  P  I  G  E  N
D  Y  W  M  G  E  U  C  C  A  T  L  C  F  A
S  N  R  X  V  I  F  B  I  W  T  A  X  Q  L
C  A  A  P  G  D  E  N  M  A  R  K  L  A  O
O  W  P  L  A  I  N  O  T  S  E  N  W  Y  P
T  Y  E  I  E  X  P  F  V  A  Z  N  I  O  E
L  B  A  T  M  C  I  D  D  G  T  B  W  A  O
A  N  K  X  B  W  I  D  W  D  S  F  K  O  C
N  X  Z  F  W  P  E  D  B  W  L  J  T  P  L
D  M  L  T  V  G  B  Z  Q  U  G  H  A  T  Z
G  V  H  B  K  H  K  F  M  K  C  C  D  P  W
P  H  M  H  F  M  X  Q  T  M  V  O  J  V  M
```

BELGIUM	SCOTLAND	ICELAND
DENMARK	SPAIN	POLAND
ITALY	ESTONIA	ARMENIA

EURO WORD SEARCH #4

Can you find the words below hidden in the grid? Words can be found horizontally, vertically, or diagonally. Keep an eye out in all directions!

```
C  B  H  H  T  S  I  A  V  C  I  U  Q  E  T
G  Z  O  T  Q  B  Z  I  H  F  F  P  D  W  S
S  L  E  A  R  S  I  B  Z  I  S  N  A  V  I
E  D  X  C  S  I  E  R  O  N  A  E  J  T  L
A  X  N  F  H  W  K  E  N  L  N  P  K  O  G
P  S  W  A  V  I  P  S  R  A  N  D  H  S  Q
N  F  F  H  L  U  A  E  T  N  H  J  N  T  Z
C  K  D  V  K  R  Z  R  Y  D  O  U  N  L  H
A  O  V  V  D  T  E  J  E  D  F  N  L  L  B
U  K  R  A  I  N  E  H  O  P  D  P  F  B  M
Z  C  P  W  G  Y  Y  O  T  Y  U  R  Z  Y  D
K  C  S  G  P  Q  I  I  W  E  A  B  M  J  W
A  Z  E  R  B  A  I  J  A  N  N  U  L  J  H
T  A  U  V  Y  D  R  G  C  W  G  J  G  I  S
F  Q  E  G  S  T  K  E  X  L  L  X  B  H  C
```

AZERBAIJAN	FRANCE	SERBIA
CZECHIA REPUBLIC	ISRAEL	SWITZERLAND
FINLAND	NETHERLANDS	UKRAINE

EURO WORD SEARCH #5

Can you find the words below hidden in the grid? Words can be found horizontally, vertically, or diagonally. Keep an eye out in all directions!

```
B U Q F O P R T N U M Q B F A
C U A Q X V K C W Q I A A V I
W A L I M P O S Z W S R C M V
L L B G F F P S K Y O S Y D T
W I M X A P U P O E J N Z U A
C M T S N R W D I K V F W U L
L C U H K T I S P W P Q L J K
X Y I H U K L A O Q V R A N B
D P L W R A T L A R B I G U D
X R A J N B N Z G R E Y U T X
X U H D S P S I R U S D H R X
L S S S X B V S A V X E Y A H
G R J B E L A R U S A X G W K
L I E C H T E N S T E I N G R
Q P A W U N X S T A C A K J H
```

BELARUS	**FAROE ISLANDS**	**LATVIA**
BULGARIA	**GIBRALTAR**	**LIECHTENSTEIN**
CYPRUS	**KOSOVO**	**LITHUANIA**

EURO WORD SEARCH #6

Can you find the words below hidden in the grid? Words can be found horizontally, vertically, or diagonally. Keep an eye out in all directions!

P	B	L	K	C	A	N	E	D	E	W	S	Q	H	R
Y	C	A	H	S	K	I	L	E	E	Z	L	U	I	S
N	W	K	E	I	F	V	N	Z	M	X	V	Z	D	Q
Z	O	W	C	R	R	M	H	O	N	R	Q	U	Y	H
I	X	R	Q	E	O	W	S	M	D	J	W	J	O	F
U	X	D	W	L	O	R	G	E	N	E	T	N	O	M
W	R	M	D	A	G	T	O	X	S	Z	C	C	Q	U
L	Y	O	O	N	Y	N	W	A	J	X	N	A	N	R
T	V	U	E	D	A	F	N	M	M	Y	Q	B	M	N
A	M	I	I	P	A	M	N	P	U	R	H	Q	G	U
R	A	R	V	Z	A	P	P	F	W	D	Y	O	H	V
A	L	G	L	R	Y	C	X	K	B	T	Z	H	T	B
J	T	M	I	M	E	U	S	A	P	K	F	F	D	O
Z	A	N	V	I	B	Z	G	E	M	A	B	G	A	Z
N	O	R	T	H	E	R	N	I	R	E	L	A	N	D

MALTA	MACEDONIA	IRELAND
MOLDOVA	NORTHERN IRELAND	SAN MARINO
MONTENEGRO	NORWAY	SWEDEN

EURO CROSSWORD #1

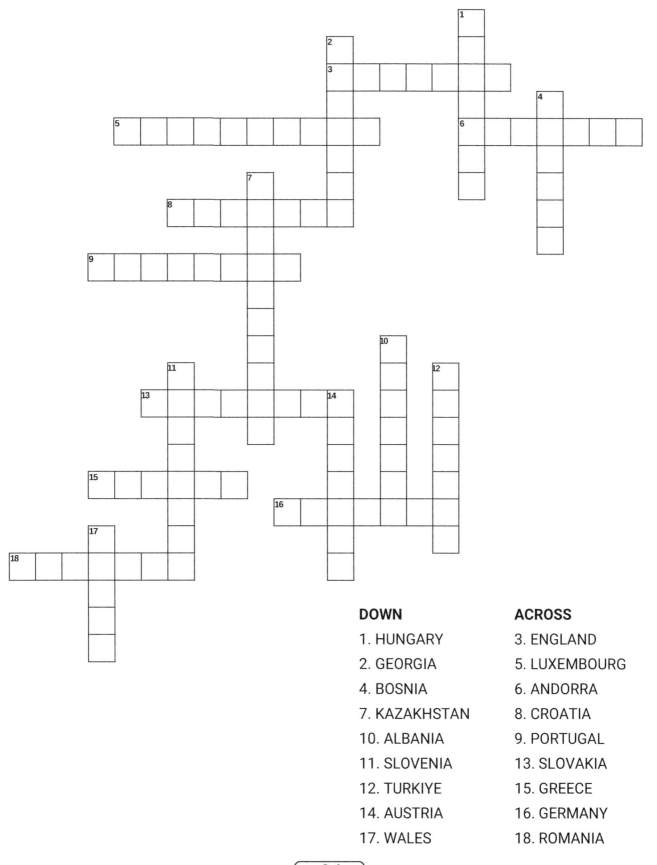

DOWN
1. HUNGARY
2. GEORGIA
4. BOSNIA
7. KAZAKHSTAN
10. ALBANIA
11. SLOVENIA
12. TURKIYE
14. AUSTRIA
17. WALES

ACROSS
3. ENGLAND
5. LUXEMBOURG
6. ANDORRA
8. CROATIA
9. PORTUGAL
13. SLOVAKIA
15. GREECE
16. GERMANY
18. ROMANIA

EURO CROSSWORD #2

ACROSS

1. SPAIN

2. ISRAEL

4. SCOTLAND

6. FINLAND

8. BELGIUM

9. FRANCE

11. DENMARK

12. ICELAND

14. SWITZERLAND

15. CZECHIA

16. UKRAINE

DOWN

1. SERBIA

3. ESTONIA

5. NETHERLANDS

7. AZERBAIJAN

10. POLAND

12. ITALY

13. ARMENIA

85

EURO MAZE

Guide the player to reach the Berlin Olympiastadion Football Stadium, where the thrilling Euro 24 final will take place.

EURO MAZE

Time for a matching adventure! Connect the same items by following the correct path. Can you navigate and match them all?

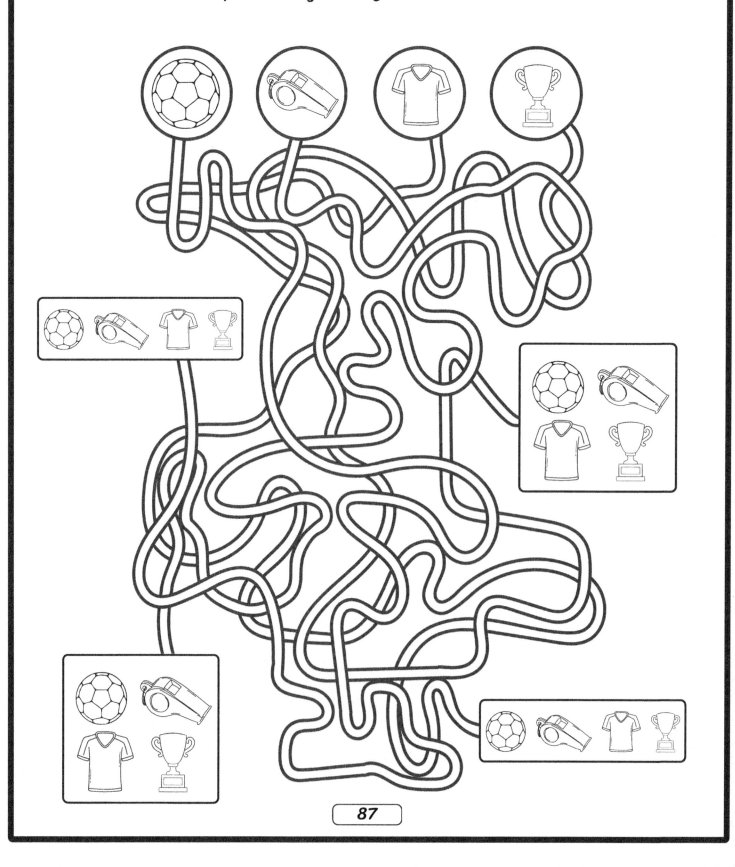

GOAL PUZZLE

Find the way to the goal by following the balls.

CREATIVITY AND DREAMING

*Get ready to design your dream player's jersey! On the front and back,
draw and colour your jersey, and don't forget to add a cool jersey number.
Let your creativity shine as you bring your dream player's outfit to life.*

CREATIVITY AND DREAMING

Time to design your dream player's shoes! Let your imagination run wild as you draw and colour the coolest pair of shoes.

CREATIVITY AND DREAMING

Draw the other side of the image by using the grid. Let your imagination shine as you complete the picture.

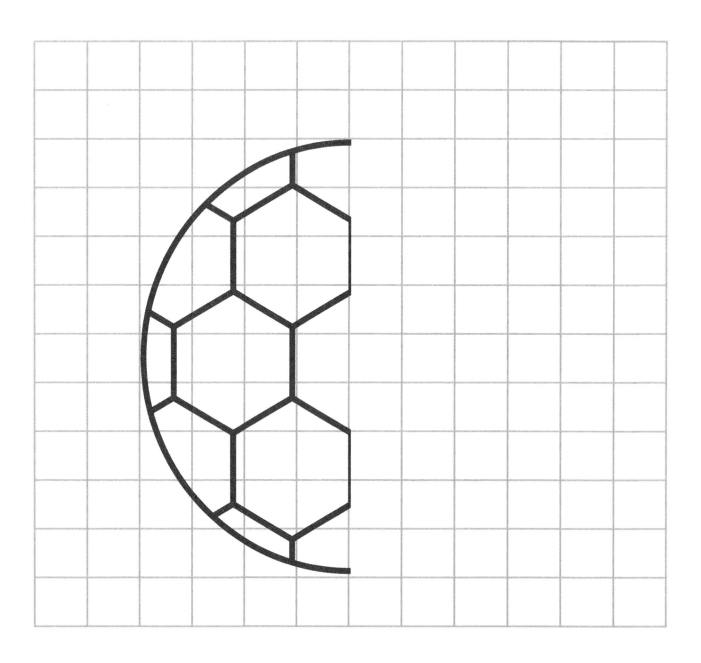

CREATIVITY AND DREAMING

Draw the other side of the image by using the grid. Let your imagination shine as you complete the picture.

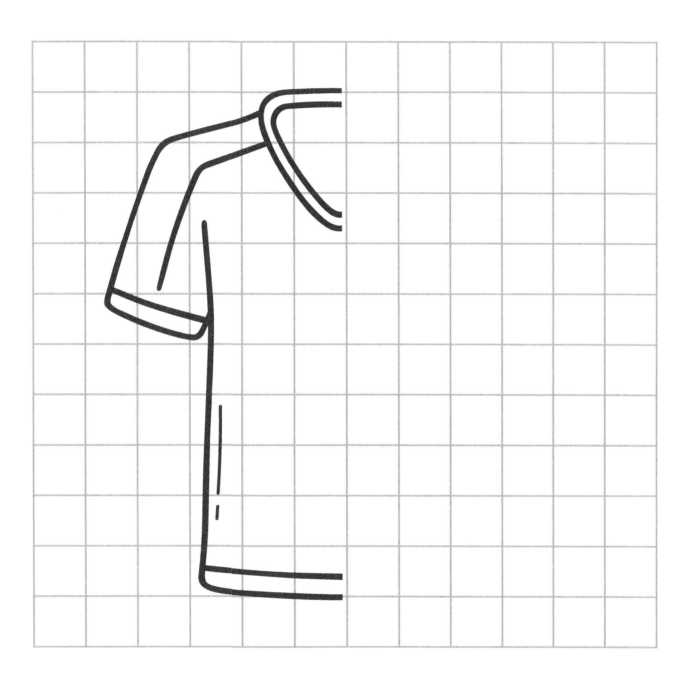

CREATIVITY AND DREAMING

Draw the other side of the image by using the grid. Let your imagination shine as you complete the picture.

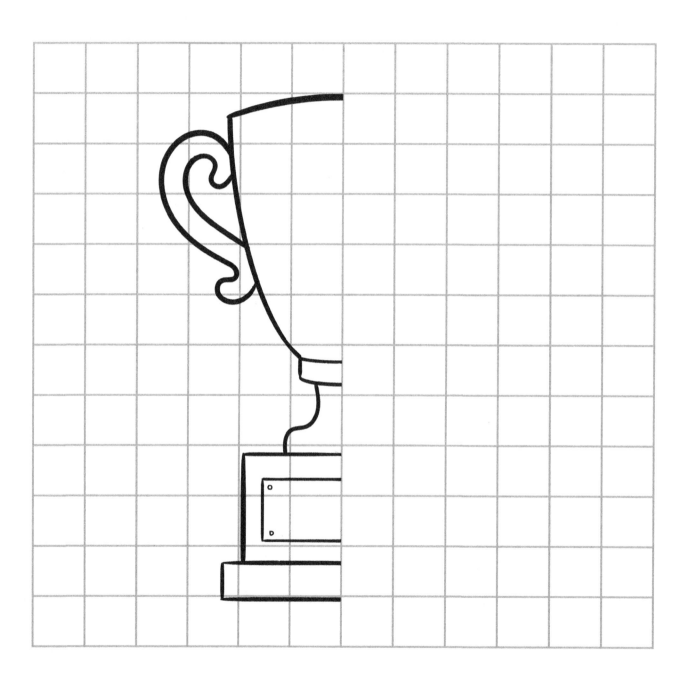

CREATIVITY AND DREAMING

Draw the other side of the image by using the grid. Let your imagination shine as you complete the picture.

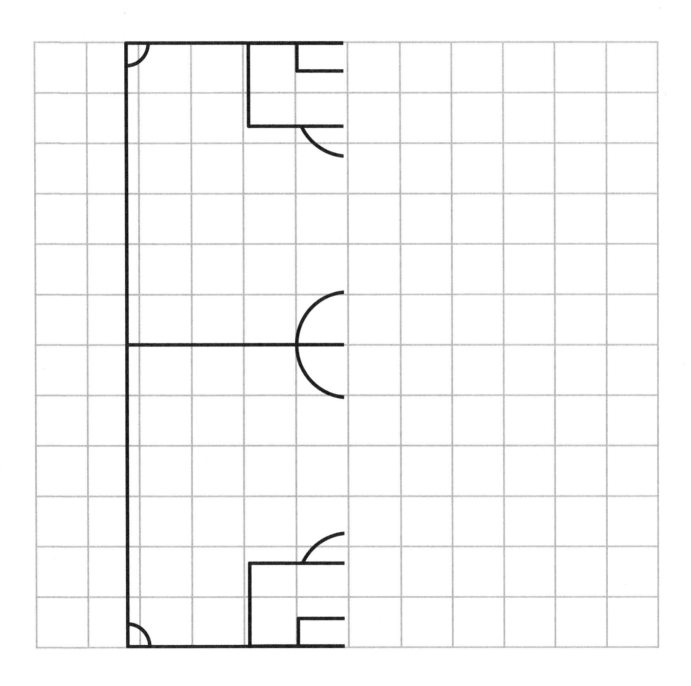

NAME MATCHING

Complete the England player's name by picking the correct last name and putting it next to the first name. Can you make the perfect matches?

- Reece _____

- Kieran _____

- Eric _____

- Conor _____

- Bukayo _____

- Ivan _____

- Kalvin _____

- James _____

- Jarrod _____

- Callum _____

- Marcus _____

- Eddie _____

- Wilson
- Phillips
- Maddison
- Nketiah

- Gallagher
- Trippier
- Bowen
- James

- Dier
- Rashford
- Toney
- Saka

NAME MATCHING

Identify the country of the given player and write the country name next to the player. Can you match them up correctly?

- Cristiano Biraghi　　_____

- Cristiano Ronaldo　　_____

- Robert Lewandowski　_____

- Kevin Trapp　　　　　_____

- Alexander Isak　　　　_____

- Radu Dragusin　　　　_____

- Attila Szalai　　　　　_____

- Giorgos Masouras　　　_____

- Antoine Griezmann　　_____

- Germany
- Hungary
- Italy
- Portugal
- France
- Romania
- Greece
- Poland
- Sweden

ANSWER KEYS

EURO WORD SEARCH #1

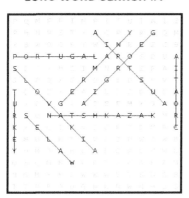

EURO WORD SEARCH #2

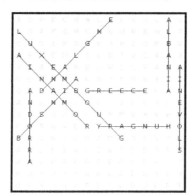

WORD SEARCH #3

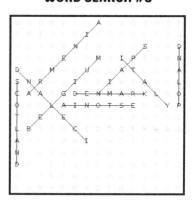

EURO WORD SEARCH #4

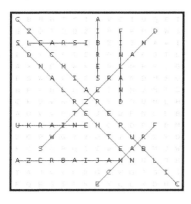

EURO WORD SEARCH #5

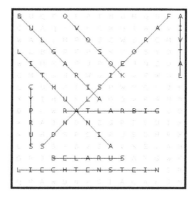

EURO WORD SEARCH #6

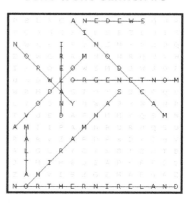

EURO CROSSWORD #1

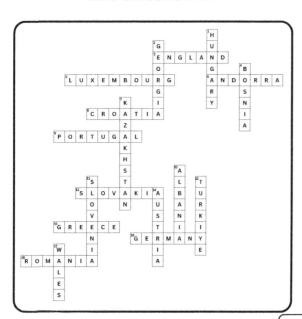

EURO CROSSWORD #2

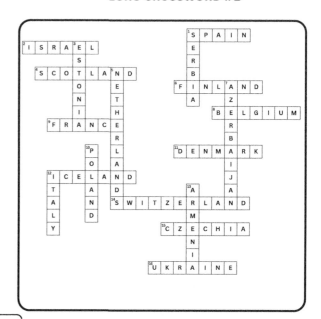

Printed in Great Britain
by Amazon

43309606R00057